ENGAGING WITH SCRIPTURE TO IMPACT OUR WORLD

"Do your best to present yourself to God as one approved, a worker who does not need to be ashamed and who correctly handles the word of truth."

2 Timothy 2:15

Philip Project Nottingham

These talks, first entitled *How to Read and Apply the Bible*, were given at the IFES Graduates' Conference for Europe and Eurasia in 2006, in Schloss Mittersill, Austria.

John Stott, then aged 85, was addressing a group of 90 young professionals, gathered from Ireland to Albania, and now embarking on a range of careers. He wanted to invest in these recent graduates for their years ahead. His desire was to give them a framework for handling Scripture, and for observing its authority; a means of using Scripture to shape their lives; and a model which they could use themselves to teach and to inspire others.

It was always John Stott's intention that the addresses be published for wider distribution. In sharing them, we honour the memory of this humble and great man of God, and carry forward the trust he placed in IFES.

STUDENTS OF THE WORD

ENGAGING WITH SCRIPTURE TO IMPACT OUR WORLD

JOHN STOTT

Foreword by Daniel Bourdanné

IFES

STUDENTS OF THE WORD
Engaging with Scripture
to Impact our World

John Stott (1921-2011)

Four addresses given at the IFES Graduates' Conference
Schloss Mittersill, Austria, 2006

First published by IFES 2013

ISBN 978-1-899464-19-7

Printed in the UK by Pennyprint, Tyne and Wear

'Where are the Timothys of the rising generation and of the new millennium? That is, where are the young men and women who will resist the pressures of the prevailing culture, who will stand firm in their commitment to the authority of Scripture, and who will spend their lives in the liberating service of the gospel? ...

'You may be young, shy and weak. So was Timothy. You may live in a hostile environment. So did Timothy. But like Timothy you have all the resources you need, in the God-breathed Scriptures of the Old Testament and in the teaching and example of the apostles in the New Testament; they can guide, equip and inspire you.'

John Stott's closing words at the IFES World Assembly 1999, Korea

The IFES community unites evangelical student movements in over 150 countries: more than half a million students on campuses worldwide who are being transformed by the redemptive power of the gospel and are sharing their faith with their friends. In the daily realities of student life, they are engaging with God's word together, developing a Christian mind in their sphere of study, and learning to integrate faith with the whole of life.

On graduation, as these believers enter the workplace, they bring Kingdom values into the public arenas, and help strengthen the witness of their local church. They are the fruit of our student ministry. They are the Timothys of their generation, and the new Daniels and Josephs, Esthers and Deborahs. In God's grace, they will influence their societies, families and communities for his glory.

John Stott was a part of this global Fellowship from his own student days in Cambridge, and he remained a wholehearted and active supporter of IFES all his life. He loved to see IFES movements equipping and enabling students to grow into 'balanced biblical Christians' and life-long disciples of Christ.

To find out more about the IFES student ministry in your country, and how God is at work among students around the world, visit ifesworld.org

Contents

Foreword

My first encounter with Uncle John was neither a head-to-head nor a face-to-face meeting. It was through the medium of a book. I was a young student in Togo when I first read *L'essentiel du Christianisme [Basic Christianity]*. Here I discovered an author who could communicate intelligently with students.

Every time I met him personally over the years to come, I was struck by his humility, and by the love and servant-heartedness he demonstrated. It did not take long for me to see how closely he identified with students, and with the whole ministry of IFES, in which he had played a major role since its founding.

His exceptional skill as a Bible expositor; his remarkable knowledge of the Bible, the world and the university; his gifts as an apologist and writer; and his friendship – all these together enabled him to influence Christian academics from all backgrounds and disciplines, in virtually every part of the world. He helped them to make the most of their intellect. He always advocated for an intelligent faith, avoiding the unbiblical dichotomy between faith and reason. He fought against anti-intellectualism. Uncle John took the world of the university seriously – undergraduate, graduate and faculty – energetically urging Christians to develop 'a Christian mind'.

Uncle John took the world of the university seriously

I will never forget receiving the news of his death on 27 July, 2011, during the IFES World Assembly in Krakow, Poland. Uncle John had joined us for these global leadership gatherings whenever he could manage it. Now, here we were, gathered around the Word of God and in the fellowship of prayer, when our dear Uncle was called home by God. He had gone to be in glory with the Lord, leaving us, the IFES family – staff and students – a powerful example. He had finished the race well.

On the second anniversary of John Stott's death, I am especially glad to publish the last talks he gave to an IFES gathering, in 2006. Here he addresses three central concerns: the nature and authority of Scripture, its interpretation, and the importance of developing a Christian mind. In an era marked by pluralism and relativism, these matters are as crucial as ever.

When the Bible is misinterpreted, it leads to distortion in doctrine and in practice. Developing a Christian mind will not only help believers to be true disciples of Jesus Christ, deeply- and wholly-rooted in the Word of God; it will also bring about conversions. I am worried by the lack of biblical knowledge and culture amongst students in the increasingly-secular global West. We must keep working to change this. Now there is a shift of the centre of gravity to the global South, to countries not traditionally known as Christian countries, with cultures shaped by other faiths, the development of the Christian mind here is an absolute necessity.

God truly inspired his servant Uncle John – pastor, visionary and prophet – to draw our attention to these matters. In these talks, he invites us to take responsibility in continuing this vital teaching. He encourages us always to give pride of place to the Word of God, defending its authority and interpreting it faithfully. For this will lead to greater maturity, and well-grounded Christian thinking. Thus I see this book as a legacy both for its content, and its symbolic value.[1]

Developing a Christian mind will help believers and bring about conversions

I have great joy in making these talks available to all the IFES national movements and more widely to the Church. Take them and read them! Where possible, meditate on them not only personally, but with your families and friends, so these things take root in individual lives and in communities.

I want to thank John Stott's Literary Executors who have graciously given permission to IFES to publish this text. I also want to thank my dear sister in Christ, Julia Cameron, for her editorial work. She has given me unstinting help at every stage towards publication. I thank, too, all those who have provided generous financial gifts to enable the book to be published. May God multiply your generosity in using it to strengthen many Christians in their faith.

May the Lord continue to speak to us through his servant Uncle John, who is still with us through his teaching and writing; and may God's name continue to be glorified through him.

Daniel Bourdanné
IFES General Secretary

Oxford, July 2013

1

The Authority of Scripture

INTRODUCTION

It's helpful to think about the authority of scripture against the background of the contemporary crises of authority – both the revolt against authority in the world and a loss of an agreed authority in the church. It is this which lies at the root of our theological confusion; one might even say our theological chaos. In theory, all Christians confess that Jesus Christ is Lord, and that the authority over the church is in his hands. So *how* does Christ speak today? *How* does he govern his church? *How* does he exercise his authority? It is here that churches disagree with one another. Let me set the context by outlining briefly four approaches, and then we shall examine more fully the evangelical convictions about scripture.

The Roman Catholic Church teaches that Christ rules through the *magisterium*, that is through the teaching authority which they believe Christ has given to the church and, indeed, supremely to the Pope and to the Bishops around him.

The Orthodox churches teach that Christ governs the church through what they call the *holy tradition* – which includes scripture.

Liberal theologians teach that Christ rules the church through what they are pleased to call the climax of educated opinion.

Anglicans, who, popularly-speaking, are always trying to find a middle road, accept the threefold cord of scripture, tradition and reason.

Evangelical people and reformed people, like ourselves, say that Christ rules the church through scripture. To be sure, tradition and reason have a vital role in the elucidation of scripture and in the application of scripture. But scripture has supreme authority in the church. That's what we believe. But the question is, why?

The authority of Christ and the authority of scripture belong together

The reason why the church has historically submitted to scripture is that our Lord Jesus Christ did so, and he urged his disciples to do the same. So the authority of Christ and the authority of scripture belong together. The church has no liberty to repudiate what our Lord has affirmed.

Our Lord Jesus lived *between* the two testaments. When he was on earth, he looked back on the Old Testament which was already complete, and he looked forward to the New Testament which had not yet begun to be written. So the ways in which he affirmed the Old and the New Testament were obviously different from one another. So we must look at them separately.

CHRIST'S ENDORSEMENT OF THE OLD TESTAMENT

We can usually understand our view of something through our use of it. And Jesus shows us his view of the Old Testament in this way. His personal submission to Old Testament scripture is very wonderful and is seen in three different spheres.

MORAL CONDUCT Jesus was determined to obey what was written of him in Old Testament scripture. No example is more impressive than his encounter with the devil in the Judean desert, where he was tempted to disobey God. Each cunning temptation was countered with an appropriate quotation from either Deuteronomy 6 or 8. 'Get behind me', Jesus said to the devil, 'because it stands written'. That single word, the Greek word *gegraptai* – it stands written in scripture – was enough to settle the issue. There was no need to discuss with the devil, there was no need to argue, there was no need to negotiate, the issue had *already* been settled by scripture. This voluntary subordination of the Son of God to the word of God is exceedingly significant. Jesus lived under its moral authority himself. If he did, surely, we should.

OFFICIAL MISSION The gospels don't reveal how Jesus came to know either who he was – his identity – or what he had come into the world to do – his mission. We must assume that he came to this conviction through meditating on scripture as God spoke to him through it. His quotations from the Old Testament seem to make plain that Jesus claimed to be both Daniel's Son of Man and Isaiah's Suffering Servant. The Son of Man came with the clouds of heaven, and the Suffering Servant died for our sins and had as his vocation to bring light to the Gentiles. Jesus fused these two images into one. As the Son of Man, he came in glory and as the Suffering Servant he died for the sins of his people. So bringing the two together, he affirmed that he *must* enter into his glory *through* his suffering and death. 'The Son of Man will go as it is written of him' (Mark 14:21). This explains Jesus' extraordinary sense of compulsion to do what was written of him in scripture.

As a boy of only twelve, he said to his parents 'Did you not know that I must' (note the compulsion: *must*) 'be in my Father's house' or 'I must be about my Father's business'. This sense of compulsion continued during his public ministry. For example, in Mark 8:31: The Son of Man *must* suffer many things and be rejected, and after three days rise again. Then it continued after his resurrection, as he said that everything *must* be fulfilled 'that is written about me in the law and the prophets' (Luke 24:44).

So why *must* these things take place? Because scripture said so. Voluntarily and deliberately, Christ put himself under the authority of scripture. He determined to fulfil scripture in his mission as in his moral standards. So when Peter tried to prevent his arrest in the Garden of Gethsemane, and drew his sword, cutting off the right ear of the High Priest's servant, Jesus said, 'Do you think that I cannot call on my Father and he will at once send more than twelve legions of angels. But how then would scripture be fulfilled that it *must* be so?' There again is the same compulsion.

> **Christ put himself under the authority of scripture**

So throughout his earthly life, as a boy of twelve, during his public ministry, and after his resurrection, he felt the steady compulsion of scripture upon him and maintained an unwavering determination to *do* what is written of him in scripture.

PUBLIC DEBATES Christ was a controversialist. He engaged in constant debate with the religious leaders of his day. They disagreed with him, and he disagreed with them. And in every question or conflict, he regarded scripture as the final court of appeal. In particular, Jesus criticised both the Pharisees and the Sadducees. He criticised the Pharisees for *adding* to scripture the traditions of the elders. And he criticised the Sadducees for *subtracting* from scripture – subtracting its supernatural element. So to the Pharisees, Jesus said: 'You have a fine way of rejecting the commandments of God by your traditions.' And to the Sadducees, he said: 'You are in error because you do not know the scriptures or the power of God.'

It is beyond question that our Lord Jesus Christ submitted to the Old Testament as the word of his heavenly Father. The decisive factor for him was what was written. That settled every uncertainty. And there is no example of Jesus contradicting scripture, only of his submitting to it and fulfilling it. You may ask: What about the six antitheses in the Sermon on the Mount, recorded in Matthew 5? ('You have heard that it was said, but I say...') There are some liberal scholars who imagine that Christ was contradicting Moses. No, he was contradicting the scribal misinterpretations and distortions of Moses. He didn't say: 'You've seen that it was written, and I say something different'. He was not contradicting what was *written* in scripture, but what was *said* (in the oral tradition). So the gospel evidence is incontrovertible. In heart and mind and life, Jesus humbly submitted to the Old Testament as to God's word written. And because Jesus did, so must we.

There are only two possible ways to escape this logic. That is to conclude Jesus was mistaken or was pretending. It's important for us to reflect on these alternatives.

Was he mistaken? The argument goes like this: 'Jesus was imprisoned by his incarnation in the limited mental reach of a first century Jew. He believed in the authority of scripture, as did all his Jewish contemporaries. But like them, he was mistaken.' This is commonly called the theory of *kenosis* – from the Greek for 'he emptied himself' (see Philippians 2:7). In short, he emptied himself of his supernatural knowledge, so would make mistakes. And among these mistakes was his erroneous view of scripture. It does seem to be true that Jesus, during his life on earth, was not omniscient, for he asked questions, which suggests that he didn't know the answers. He specifically said that he did not know the day or hour of his return (Mark 13:32). Only the Father knew the date of the second coming. On the other hand, he knew what he didn't know. He wasn't ignorant of his limits. And knowing the limits of his knowledge, he stayed within those limits and never strayed beyond them. While he was not omniscient, he was inerrant. He taught only what his Father had given him to teach and hence he made no mistakes. So his teaching of the Old Testament was not *mistaken*. It was true.

Was he pretending? The argument goes like this: 'Jesus knew perfectly well that scripture was not infallible. But because his contemporaries believed it was, and because he didn't want to upset them, he went along with their error. He pretended to hold it as well.' This is the accommodation theory: that he deliberately *accommodated* himself to their view.

This theory is equally intolerable. To attribute to Jesus Christ a conscious deception is a slander upon him and upon his integrity. It is derogatory to him. He never hesitated to disagree with his contemporaries if he believed them to be mistaken. He criticised their views on tradition, on the Sabbath, on fasting, and he rejected their political notion of messiahship. So why should he not dissent from their view of scripture if he didn't agree with it? The accommodation theory would make Jesus guilty of the sin he most detested, and that is the sin of hypocrisy.

Here are two attempted escape routes both of which declared his teaching to be mistaken. According to the first, Jesus' mistake was involuntary, he couldn't help it, he was imprisoned in the mentality of a first century Jew. According to the second, his mistake was deliberate. He chose to pretend that he agreed with his contemporaries when he didn't. According to the first, he was deceived, according to the second, he was a deceiver. Both *kenosis* and *accommodation* must be firmly rejected. They seriously discredit the honesty, integrity and authority of the Son of God. Against these slanderous speculations we hold that Jesus knew what he was saying – and he meant it – and it is true. So we must believe and teach it as well.

CHRIST'S INTENTION FOR THE NEW TESTAMENT

Now we move from Christ's endorsement of the Old Testament to the authority of the New Testament and Christ's *provision* for it.

Jesus not only *foresaw* the writing of the New Testament scripture – parallel to the scriptures of the Old Testament – but he *intended* it, for the same reason, namely to record and interpret what God was doing. And so he made provision for it by appointing and equipping his apostles, some of whom would write it.

The word *apostolos* means simply one who was sent. It is used in the New Testament in three different ways.

First, for all of us. There is one sense in which all Christians are in apostolic ministry, sent into the world; but only in one case is this term used for such. (See John 13: 16 'he who is sent is not greater than he who sent him'.) As the Father sent the Son into the world, so the Son sends us into the world to share the gospel with the world. All of us are part of the apostolic mission (*apostolos*) of the church.

All of us are part of the apostolic mission of the church

Secondly, two or three times in the New Testament, it is used of people who are called 'apostles of the churches' (NB not 'apostles of Christ'). In your church you perhaps call them mission partners. In 2 Corinthians 8:23 they are described as 'representatives' of the churches. These people are sent out by the churches on a mission or an errand of some kind. We see in Philippians 2:25 that Epaphroditus, an apostle of the church of Philippi, is called 'your messenger' or 'your representative'.

Thirdly, of the overwhelming use of the word *apostolos* in the New Testament, there is the unique group we call the Twelve (apostles) to whom were later added the apostle Paul and probably the apostle James. These are rightly called apostles of Christ.

Please note with me the double background of the word apostle: a prophetic background from the prophets of the Old Testament, and a rabbinic background.

Let's look at the prophetic background. The Old Testament prophets were described as being sent by Jahweh. 'I am sending you!' God said to Moses in Exodus 3. Or again to Isaiah: 'Whom shall I send, and who will go for us?' And to Jeremiah: 'You must go to everyone to whom I send you!' We notice the language of sending that comes again and again. And God also said through

Jeremiah to the Israelites: 'Day after day and again and again I sent to you my servants, the prophets'. The same language is also used of the false prophets. God said, for example: 'They are prophesying lies in my name, I did not send them.' They are not genuine prophets because I did not send them. So then just as Jahweh sent his prophets to speak to Israel in his name, so Jesus sent out the Twelve to speak and preach in his name. The Twelve were the New Testament equivalent of the Old Testament prophets, and they were equally inspired.

Now to the Rabbinic background for the term apostle, from the so called *shaliach* of Rabbinic Judaism.

The *shaliach* was sent out by the Sanhedrin (the Supreme Jewish Council), especially to teach the Jews of the Diaspora. This was a trusted role, and the *shaliach*, representing the Sanhedrin, commanded serious respect. Listen to this very important little phrase in the Greek: 'the one sent by a person is as this person himself.' In other words, he carries with him the authority of the sending body. Knowing this of the prophet and the *shaliach*, Jesus deliberately chose the title apostle for the Twelve. We read 'He called his disciples to him, and chose twelve of them, whom he also designated *apostles*.' (Luke 6:13) They were his spokesmen, they were his ambassadors, they were his authorized representatives, and he sent them out saying: 'He who listens to you, listens to me. He who rejects you, rejects me.'

Having seen this double background of the word apostolos, I want to ask you to notice the fourfold uniqueness of the apostles of Christ, so we keep them separate in our minds from ordinary Christians or the apostles of the churches.

Fourfold uniqueness of Christ's apostles

1. **Personal appointment and authorization by Jesus.** We've seen how he chose the Twelve and gave them his authority. He gave the same authority to Paul, on the Damascus road. Jesus said to him: *Ego apostello se* – I apostle you. There, in that moment of conversion, came his commissioning as Christ made him an *apostle*. He chose him, sent him and authorized him. In nine out of the thirteen letters of Paul in the New Testament, we read 'Paul, an apostle of Jesus Christ, according to the will (or commandment)

of God'. Whereas Timothy was called a brother, he was not called an apostle. So this personal appointment and authorization by Jesus himself is where we begin.

2. **Eyewitness experience of Jesus.** Christ appointed twelve to be with him (Mark 3:14). These twelve had unequalled opportunities to hear his words, to see his works and so to bear witness to what they had seen and heard. In the upper room (John 15:27) Jesus said to them: 'you also shall bear witness because you have been with me from the beginning.' We remember Peter's words when Judas was replaced by Matthias: a major criterion was to choose someone 'who has accompanied us during all the time that the Lord Jesus went in and out among us' and 'who must be, with us, a witness to the resurrection' (Acts 1:21ff). So this is why Paul could be an apostle, as could James, because he'd seen the risen Lord.

   In 1 Corinthians 9:1 Paul says: 'Am I not an apostle? Have I not seen Jesus, our Lord?' And then in the context of the list of the resurrection appearances, he writes 'and last of all he appeared also to me, and I am the least of the apostles.' (1 Corinthians 15:8). Here he claims again to have seen the risen Lord. So that's why we need to have the courage to say that there are no apostles in the church today. There are bishops, there are superintendents, there are leaders, missionaries of different kinds, and church planters – but there is nobody with the authority of the apostle Paul, or the apostle John or the apostle Peter – they are unique and must be given their uniqueness. So there is no apostolic succession. The only apostolic succession we protestants believe in is a succession or continuation of apostolic teaching as it has come down to us in the New Testament. So the apostolic succession is the New Testament, bequeathed to the church.

   There is no apostolic succession

3. **Extraordinary inspiration by the Holy Spirit.** Jesus gave the apostles, in the upper room, two particular promises not made to anybody else.

   > 'When the Spirit of Truth is come, he will remind you of everything I have said to you.' (John 14:26)

'I have much more to say to you, but you cannot bear it now.' (John 16:12f) In other words, I cannot complete my teaching ministry, because of your lack of understanding. But when the Holy Spirit comes, he will lead you into all the truth. He will complete my teaching ministry.

The first promise about reminding them of what he has said to them was surely fulfilled in the writing of the gospels. The second promise, 'that I will lead you into all truth' must have been fulfilled in the writing of the epistles.[2]

4. **Their ability to work miracles.** The whole subject of biblical miracles is too big to go into here. Let's just look at 2 Corinthians 12:12 where the apostle Paul says that the marks of a true apostle (ie those which identify a true apostle) were shown through signs and wonders and miracles. So Paul claims that his miracles were the signs of a true apostle.

Now we turn from the uniqueness of the apostles to look at how they and others recognized this uniqueness.

First, it was recognized by Christ himself. 'He who receives you, receives me' said Christ. (Matthew 10:40)

Secondly, it was recognized by the apostles themselves. There is a self-conscious apostolic authority shining throughout their letters. The apostles did not write in the name of the church, they wrote in the name of Christ to the church. They required their letters to be read in the public assembly (Colossians 4:16), alongside the scriptures of the Old Testament. Consider the extraordinary language of authority with which Paul writes in 2 Thessalonians 'Now, I command you, brethren, in the name of the Lord Jesus Christ, that you keep away from certain brothers... and that you obey what is written in this letter.'[3] Nobody in the church today issues such commands, not even the Pope! This is an indication of Paul's unique apostolic authority, his self-conscious apostolic authority. Perhaps the most extraordinary example of his apostolic authority is in Galatians. When he visited the Galatian cities on his first missionary journey, he was sick so had to leave high ground in the tour of

Apostolic authority is shining throughout their letters

the mountains in order to recuperate. And he says: 'Although my illness was a trial to you, you did not despise me; instead you Galatians welcomed me as if I were an angel of God and as if I were Christ Jesus himself.'[4] He doesn't rebuke them. He doesn't tell them that they've got no right to treat him as if he were an angel or as if he were Christ Jesus. He allows them to recognize his authority as an apostle of Christ. This is indeed an amazing statement.

Thirdly, it was recognized by the early church. Bishop Ignatius of Antioch in Syria was on his way from Antioch[5] to Rome to be martyred, when he wrote seven letters to the churches. Those to the churches in Tralles[6], Rome and Smyrna have survived. In several places he wrote: 'I do not issue you with commands like Peter or Paul for I am not an apostle but a condemned man.' Again, a remarkable statement. He distinguished himself from the apostles.

My last example is the New Testament Canon. The early church saw the need to finalize the New Testament Canon because they recognized that some books had authority while others did not. The test they brought was apostolicity. They asked themselves: 'Was this book written by an apostle? And if not, does it contain the teaching of the apostles? Does it carry the authority of the apostles?' If so, it was admitted into the canon of the New Testament and accepted as apostolic.' In short, the test of canonicity was apostolicity.

The 1958 Lambeth Conference, the ten-yearly gathering of all Bishops in the Anglican Communion, summed this up in these words: 'The Church is not 'over' the holy scriptures, but 'under' them, in the sense that the process of canonization was not one whereby the Church *conferred* authority on the books, but one whereby the Church *acknowledged* them to possess authority. To that apostolic authority the Church must ever bow.'

And why? The books were recognized as giving the witness of the Apostles to the life, teaching, death and resurrection of the Lord Jesus Christ and the interpretation by the Apostles of these events. There is the church bowing down before the authority of the apostles.

IN SUMMARY

Our Lord Jesus Christ repeatedly endorsed the authority of the Old Testament by appealing to it, and by submitting to its authority. Secondly, our Lord Jesus Christ deliberately provided for the writing of the New Testament by appointing and equipping the apostles to speak and teach in his name. Thus both the Old Testament and the New Testament in their different ways bear the stamp of his authority. And therefore, if we would submit to the authority of Christ, we must submit to the authority of scripture. If we wish to hear the voice of Christ, we must listen to scripture through which he speaks. For the authority of scripture and the authority of Christ go together.

> **The authority of scripture and the authority of Christ go together**

The ultimate question before the church in every age is: Who is the Lord? Is the church the Lord of Jesus Christ, so that it has liberty to edit and manipulate his teaching? Or is Jesus Christ the Lord of the church, so that it must believe and obey him? Since Jesus Christ is Lord, there should be no hesitation about our answer to that question. We must accept the authority of scripture.

2

Basic Principles of Biblical Interpretation

There are many people who say that you can make the Bible teach anything you like. I agree with them. You can make the Bible teach anything you like if you are unscrupulous. But if you are diligent in the proper use of the principles of biblical interpretation, you will find that scripture controls you.

There are three foundation principles we need to grasp. They arise logically from the kind of book the Bible is, and from the kind of God it declares him to be. They depend on the basic Christian affirmation that God has spoken. Unlike the idols with which Israel was surrounded, our God is a living God. The idols, being dead, did not speak. But God has spoken. The true and the living God has spoken. So here are the three principles in brief.

God spoke in order to be understood
(the principle of simplicity).

God spoke in precise and particular historic contexts,
never in a vacuum (the principle of history).

God spoke without contradicting himself
(the principle of harmony)

GOD SPOKE IN ORDER TO BE UNDERSTOOD

The principle of simplicity is very elementary. 'God is light, and in him is no darkness at all.' (1 John 1:5) In other words: God delights to reveal himself. In fact, it is just as much the nature of God to reveal himself, as it is the nature of light to shine. Light shines, God speaks. The purpose of speech is intelligible communication. He is a speaking God. He is not only communicative by nature, but he has communicated with us in words.

So we read: 'Your word is a lamp to my feet and a light to my path.' (Psalm 119:105) It shows me the way to go. God spoke in order for us to understand his ways. This is our foundational confidence as we approach scripture together. The Bible, my friends, is not shrouded in mist or fog. It is not a book of riddles and puzzles. God has given it, his word, to us to enlighten us. Hence what the 16th century reformers used to call the perspicuity of scripture – this was the word they used to indicate its transparency, its see-through or luminous quality.

The Bible is not a book of riddles and puzzles

Not everything in scripture is equally plain. The apostle Peter writes that there are some things in Paul's letters which are hard to understand. And if Peter couldn't always understand Paul, it would be immodest for us to claim that we can. What the reformers meant by the perspicuity of scripture is that the central message of the Bible is plain enough for anybody to understand, namely that salvation is by grace alone, in Christ alone, through faith alone.

As we read, we should look for the plain, obvious, natural meaning of the text. The Reformers sometimes called this the literal meaning. They did not mean that it was literal as opposed to figurative, for much of scripture is clearly metaphor or allegory. Let me quote Luther: 'We should stick to just the plain, natural meaning of the words as yielded by the rules of grammar and by the habits of speech which God has created among men.'

But this soon raises a question, for the natural sense of a text is not always the literal sense. It is sometimes the figurative. It's a question often of literary genre – of the kind of literature that we're handling as to whether it's literal or figurative. So I want now to give you several examples to drum this home to all of us. I wish someone had given it to me when I was a young and immature Christian. It really is very important.

Jesus' own use of vivid imagery

Christ rebuked his contemporaries on several occasions for their excessive biblical literalism.

For example in John 3, he told Nicodemus that he had to be born again. Nicodemus was evidently perplexed when he asked, 'Can a man re-enter his mother's womb and be born again?' Jesus said in effect: 'Don't be such a biblical literalist! I'm not talking about a literal, physical rebirth, but a spiritual birth.'

'Don't be such a biblical literalist!'

In John 4 we have Jesus' well-known conversation with the Samaritan woman. He told her that if she knew who it was who was speaking to her, she would have asked him for living water. She responded: 'But you haven't got a bucket, and the well is deep!' And he said to her, too, in effect: 'Don't be such a biblical literalist. I'm not talking about wells and buckets. I'm talking about the water of life. And unless you drink that, you cannot have eternal life.'

In John 6 Jesus says: 'Unless you eat the flesh of the Son of God and drink his blood, you have no life in you!' But how can this man give us his flesh to eat, they ask.

Again and again Christ brought them back from literalism to something that was figurative. That was Jesus' own use of imagery.

Anthropomorphisms in Scripture

Anthropos is the Greek word for man, and *morphe* is the Greek word for a form. Anthropomorphism in this context is to speak of God in the form of a man. The biblical authors use such expressions frequently: They talk of God's ears and his eyes, and his breath and his arm, his hands and fingers and feet, and even his nostrils. Yet Jesus said that God is spirit and if God is spirit, he has no eyes or ears or nostrils, he has no bodily parts literally. You may remember that in 2 Chronicles 16:9 it is written that the eyes of the Lord run to and fro throughout the whole earth, to show his strength on behalf of those who trust in him. When we read this, we are not to imagine a couple of divine eyes galloping over the surface of the earth! No, we are to understand that God is watchful, and will come to the aid of his people as they trust him.

Poetic passages

Psalm 19:4,5 goes like this: 'In the heavens, God has pitched a tent for the sun to live in which is like a bridegroom coming forth from his pavilion, like a champion rejoicing to run his course.' Here, within the compass of one and a half verses only, the heavens are likened to a tent for the sun to live in, and the sun in turn is likened to a bridegroom coming forth from his pavilion, and like a champion athlete, to run his course. In just a few words, then, the sun is likened to a tent-dweller, a bridegroom and an athlete. It's obvious that this is poetry and not prose. And the statement that the sun runs across the sky does not commit us to a pre-Copernican view of the universe. This is a figure of speech – it is *not* a scientific statement.

Apocalyptic literature

The Book of Revelation is sometimes referred to as 'the Apocalypse' as it is apocalyptic literature, full of weird and wonderful imagery. We read of a great red dragon, of monsters who emerge from the earth and from the sea, of a lamb as if it had been slain and so on. We must be cautious as to how we interpret these images. For example, in Revelation 7:9ff we are told that the redeemed people of God are standing before his throne wearing white robes. And who are these? Well, these are they, ‘who have come out of the great tribulation’ (a description of the Christian life) ‘and have washed their clothes and made them white with the blood of the lamb’. I’ve never attempted to launder my clothing in lamb’s blood, but I’m quite sure that if I did, my shirts would not come out white. This is not meant literally. It is a reference to the atoning death of Jesus Christ; those who put their trust in him as their Saviour will be made righteous (clean) and fit to stand before his throne.

The question of perspective

We are now moving into matters a little bit more controversial, and we’ll see whether I’ll carry you with me or not. The biblical authors record things again and again from the ordinary viewpoint of a human observer, and that’s the way we still speak today – from a human perspective. For example, we still speak of the sun rising and of the sun setting although we know it does neither – it only appears to do so, from the perspective of those who live on earth. This question of perspective throws light on the use of words like *every* and *all*. I want to suggest that they are not necessarily absolute words. They may be relative to the narrator.

Let’s look at the Flood. Some Christians insist from scripture that the Flood was universal. But does it teach that? In Genesis 7:19 we read that all the high mountains under the whole heaven were covered. Did that include Mount Fuji and Mount Denali and Mount Kilimanjaro and even Mount Everest? The question of the exact extent of the Flood will in the end be settled only by scientists. My point is that the biblical narrative does not require us to believe in a universal flood, but rather in a very extensive one in the Middle East. Similarly in Genesis 41:57 we read that ‘all the countries’ came to Egypt to buy grain from Joseph because the famine was severe ‘in all the world’. This clearly refers to the known world. Joseph and his brothers would not have had knowledge of the whole world as we now know it.

In Luke 2:1 we read that ‘all the world’ went to be enrolled in the census that the emperor had commanded. All, every nation under heaven. In Acts 2:5 we read that every nation under heaven was represented on the day of Pentecost in Jerusalem. But Luke clearly does not intend us to include in this Australian aborigines and New Zealand Maoris and the Inuit. Rather, verses 9-11 list fifteen groups to which he is referring, all gathered round the Mediterranean basin and part of the Roman Empire.

In Colossians 1:23 Paul affirmed that the gospel has been proclaimed 'to every creature under heaven'. But we know it hadn't. Paul had proclaimed the gospel in four Roman provinces: Galatia, Asia, Macedonia and Achaia. But he had not proclaimed it all over the world.

The early chapters of Genesis

Are we to understand these as literal or are we to understand them as figurative? *Some* features of Genesis 2 and 3 are surely not intended to be taken literally. For example, we will not find the tree of life in a textbook of dendrology (a textbook of trees). And we shall not find the serpent in a textbook of herpetology (the science of reptiles and amphibians). The Tree of Life and the Serpent reappear later in the Bible, especially in the Book of Revelation, where they are clearly not literal but symbolical.

But while this is true of the Tree of Life and of the Serpent, the Devil, it is emphatically not true of Adam and Eve. We must insist on the historicity of Adam and Eve. This is partly because Jesus himself said that in the beginning God made the man and the woman, but especially because Paul draws a very careful analogy or parallel between Adam and Christ. Romans 5:19 is an essential verse when we're thinking about the historicity of Adam and Eve: 'As through the disobedience of one man, Adam, many were made sinners, so through the obedience of one man, Christ, many will be made righteous.' Paul's whole argument depends on the historicity of this parallel between Adam and Jesus, between the disobedience of the one and the obedience of the other. The New Testament insists on the historicity of Adam and Eve.

We must insist on the historicity of Adam and Eve

So there is this qualification as we look for the simple, natural meaning of the text. It is sometimes figurative and not literal.

GOD SPOKE IN PARTICULAR CONTEXTS

We move on now to look at the principle of history: how God spoke in precise and particular contexts. Indeed, the chief principle of God's self-revelation is this - that he did not shout from a distance. He came down to our level when he was revealing himself, entered our situation, our context. He contextualized his message and spoke in the local language.

This principle of history is true for the incarnation of the Son of God, taking on our human flesh, and for the inspiration of scripture in which God spoke in our languages. He *condescended* or *stooped* to our level, to communicate with us. As the great C H Spurgeon, the Baptist pastor at the end of the 19th century, once said: 'Remember Jesus said: 'Feed my lambs, not my giraffes!' We too must follow the apostle Peter in teaching in a way which engages people, at their level.

A text means what its author meant

The principle of history makes us look for the *original sense* of the text as intended by the author, and as understood by the first readers. I want to quote from Professor E D Hirsch, of the University of Virginia[8] in a very simple statement which I very much hope you will take away with you. I think it's one of the most important simplicities about interpreting the Bible. In his 1967 book entitled *Validity in Interpretation* he states a simple principle: 'A text means what its author meant.' The author of a text establishes its meaning. And what it meant when it was first written or spoken, it still means today. The meaning of a text never changes; its message may change, and it may have different implications and applications, but the meaning of the text is always the same. A text means what its author originally meant.

This is where we part company with Rudolf Bultmann, the existential New Testament scholar.[9] Bultmann would say: 'A text means what it means to me, and what it means to you.' The postmodern view is that a text is 'infinitely interpretable', a phrase heard now in academia. But we say: No, it may be infinitely *applicable* but it is *not* infinitely interpretable. The meaning of a text is established by its author. That being so, our responsibility is to ask what the author meant in his writing, what he was intending to say, and how he intended his readers to understand this. It is important to recognise the difference between the words *exegesis* and *eisegesis*. (See pp 39-40.)

GOD DID NOT CONTRADICT HIMSELF

The principle of harmony rests on God speaking coherently, and we must not attribute to God the muddles and confusions which characterise our own minds. For God knows his mind, and his mind is an integrated mind; his message an integrated message. What we find in scripture is a combination of diversity and unity.

God's revelation is wonderfully rich in its diversity – both in theological emphasis and also in the media, the literary *genres*, used to convey his message. In spite of its diversity, God's self-revelation is consistent throughout. As we read in the first verses of Hebrews, it is the same God who spoke to the fathers through the prophets 'who has spoken to us in these last days in and through his Son' (Hebrews 1:1-2).

The two revelations are harmonious with one another, and the overall purpose of this revelation is recognisably the same. God's purpose is salvation. That is, to call out a people for himself, to adopt them into his family, to transform them into the image of his Son and then to send them back into the world as his witnesses and his servants; and finally to bring them and the universe to ultimate glory. So salvation is a big word. It includes the totality of God's purpose in Christ, which is why scripture bears witness to him, as he himself said.

Progressive or 'cumulative' revelation

God's revelation has been cumulative – not in the sense that he later contradicted what he had earlier taught, but rather that he has amplified it. Wise parents and teachers never teach their children at one stage what they need to contradict later. Because if they do this, for example insisting on the reality of Santa Claus and denying his reality later, they lose credibility as teachers.

As an example let me take the doctrine of the Trinity. In contrast to the polytheism of the tribes and nations that were surrounding Israel, the Old Testament emphasis is on the unity of God. So we read: 'The Lord our God is one Lord, and you shall love the Lord with all your mind, soul, heart and strength.'[12]

While there are many hints of plurality in the Old Testament, the major teaching of the Old Testament is on the unity of the Godhead. The New Testament has a different emphasis, namely the Trinity. But the New Testament authors are able to teach on the doctrine of the Trinity only *after* God's people have grasped his *unity*. They had to grasp the unity first, and then they would understand the diversity. Those are not in contradiction to one another, as we all know because we believe in the Trinity. As Luther wrote so pithily: 'We read the Bible forwards, but can only understand it backwards.' That is allowing the New Testament to interpret the Old.

'We read the Bible forwards, but can only understand it backwards'

Now, the modern theological fashion in universities is to emphasise the diversity of God's revelation, and even dare to say that there is no unity. We have, it is said, the teaching of John or James or Peter, but there is no unity. Now certainly we glory in the diversity of scripture but *not* at the expense of its unity. As Paul wrote: 'There is one body, one spirit, one Lord, one faith, one baptism, one God and Father of us all.'[13] That is the unity within diversity. Professor A M Hunter of Aberdeen University[14] wrote: 'There is a deep unity in the New Testament which dominates and transcends all the diversities.' And I hope you agree with that as I do. God has given us in scripture a revelation which is comprehensive, coherent and harmonious. And therefore we need to study the *whole* of scripture and learn to interpret each text in the light of all. This is the principle of harmony.

This will mean renouncing as deadly two common evangelical practices:

Random-dipping into Scripture. You may know the story of the young man who is in great perplexity about his future and who, because of his perplexity, resorted to random-dipping. What he came up with was 'Judas went and hanged himself.' And because that wasn't very promising, he tried again, and he got: 'Go and do thou likewise.' And because that wasn't very helpful he tried a third time, and he got: 'What you're doing, do quickly!' I am glad to report that the story goes on to tell us that this cured him of random-dipping. The ending would otherwise have been very grim!

Our ancestors in many cultures kept what they called promise boxes. These promise boxes were little scrolls of parchment, on each was written a biblical promise that had no relevance to other biblical promises. These were drawn out from the box for spiritual encouragement, in a genuine desire to please God by taking him at his word. Sometimes God condescends to our folly and gives us guidance in this way, but scripture is not an anthology of unrelated sentences. So we ought not to try God with his word. Let us renounce random-dipping.

We have to keep together dignity and depravity because scripture teaches both

Proof-texting. This is imagining that an issue can be settled by quoting a single text and ignoring the rest of the Bible. Sometimes perhaps it can, but not normally. God's revelation in any given subject is much richer and much broader than can be found in a single text. Hence our need for comprehensive study in the whole, and comprehensive exposition in the pulpit.

This brings me to two corresponding responsibilities, namely to synthesize and to harmonize.

To synthesize is to combine several parts into a single whole. Much imbalance in Christianity comes from the selective use of scripture. For example, we cannot develop a true biblical view of human beings, namely the image of God, if we concentrate entirely on their depravity and say nothing of their dignity. We have to keep together dignity and depravity because scripture teaches both. Or again we should never develop a proper biblical view of the state if we stay in Romans 13 where the state is said to be the servant of God, and forget Revelation 13 where the state has become an ally of the devil. We must work at developing a balanced, biblical Christianity. Without knowing scripture and being able to harmonize and synthesize, we shall always remain unbalanced.

It is often said that the Bible is full of contradictions. And to be sure, it does contain some apparent discrepancies. It is possible to handle these in a way that is compatible with intellectual integrity. For if we believe in the divine origin and inspiration of scripture, we will be wise not to accuse the biblical authors prematurely of being mistaken, nor of manipulating the text into a contrived unity. We must seek a natural harmonization which respects both sides of the debate. As we do this, it's especially helpful to discern the author's theological purpose.

The best example of the need for harmonization is in how to handle the conflict between the teaching of James and Paul. Paul affirmed justification by faith alone, James affirmed justification by works, and not by faith only. It is for this reason that Luther referred to the Epistle of James as 'the epistle of straw'.[15] But what was the theological *purpose* of Paul and James? It is this which permits us a harmonization. For Paul and James were both responding to different theological deviations. I think we can understand this: Paul was opposing *Judaizers* who taught justification by works. James was opposing *intellectuals* who taught that justification is but a barren orthodoxy and not a true faith. To *Judaizers* Paul insisted that we are justified not by works but by faith. To *intellectuals* James insisted that we are justified not by a barren faith, but by a faith which works.

Both Paul and James verify the nature of an authentic faith, namely a living trust which issues in good works. So James 2:18 reads: 'I will show you my faith by my works.' While Galatians 5:6 reads: 'Faith works through love.' Both apostles taught that an authentic faith works: Paul emphasized the faith which issues in works, while James emphasized the works which issue from faith. This may be harmonized. It is better to confess our ignorance as to how to harmonize, than to accuse the biblical authors of inaccuracy or error.

Scripture, then, is a coherent and organic whole which we rightly call the word of God. It is the word of God through the words of men. It issued from one divine mind and mouth although it was mediated through many minds and many mouths. Because of this double authorship of scripture – God speaking through human authors – we would expect *a priori* a combination of diversity and unity: diversity because of the many human authors, and unity because of the single divine author. This is exactly what we find.

A FRIEND AND A FOE

Exegesis and Eisegesis

The discipline of exegesis

Biblical exegesis, which derives from the principle of history, is a discipline requiring (i) integrity, in refusing to twist scripture, and (ii) sensitivity, in using our imagination to recover the situation in which the author actually found himself. We then have to struggle to rid our minds of modern perspectives. We need to think ourselves back into our author's situation and to re-create his historical context; to understand his language as he used it and as his hearers would have understood him. Calvin who was, in my view, the greatest exegete that God has yet given to the church, once wrote: 'The first business of an interpreter is to let his author say what he does say.' That's true exegesis.

Similarly, centuries later, came the great Charles Simeon, one of my personal heroes, who was vicar of Holy Trinity Church, Cambridge, for 54 years at the end of the 18th century and beginning of the 19th century.[10] One could describe him as a kind of original founder of UCCF in the UK, and through that, arguably, of IFES. He had an enormous influence on generations of students in Britain. He once wrote to his publisher these words: 'My endeavour is to bring out of scripture what is there – and not to thrust in what I think might be there. I have a great jealousy on this head: Never to speak more or less than I believe to be the mind of the Spirit in the passage I am expounding.'[11]

> **Charles Simeon had an enormous influence on generations of students in Britain**

In Christ's conversation with Nicodemus, Jesus told Nicodemus that no one can enter the kingdom of God unless he be born of water and of the spirit (John 3:5).This reference born of water is interpreted by many commentators as referring to the sacrament of baptism. But it can't refer to baptism, because baptism was not instituted until after the resurrection. Surely Jesus was referring specifically to the ministry of

John the Baptist. Nicodemus could not receive the spirit without first submitting to his baptism of repentance. John the Baptist said, 'I baptise with water but he will baptise with the Holy Spirit.' So the contrast between water and spirit was already popular in the teaching of John the Baptist. This follows the principle of history.

This work to discover the author's intention, his own context of language, is commonly referred to as grammatical-historical exegesis. It's a combination of grammar, the language, and the meaning of the text.

The folly of eisegesis

The worst blunder we can commit in our reading of scripture is to import into the text our alien ideas of a later generation. To read our 21st century thoughts back into the minds of the biblical authors, and then to claim their patronage for our opinions. So *eisegesis* is reading into the text what you would like to find there, that isn't actually there.

An American scholar, H J Cadbury, wrote a book in 1937 called *The Peril of Modernizing Jesus* – by which he meant the peril of reconstructing Jesus in our own image and not allowing him to be himself as he was. Then we could create Jesus the ascetic, Jesus the revolutionary, Jesus the capitalist, Jesus the socialist, Jesus Christ Superstar or Jesus the founder of modern business. The founder of modern business, you ask quizzically. In 1929, Bruce Barton, a Madison Avenue advertising executive, wrote a book called *The Man Nobody Knows*. The last chapter is entitled *The Founder of Modern Business*. Surely we remember that when Jesus was a boy of twelve, he said: 'Did you not know that I must be about my Father's business?'

This book, which didn't profit me at all, is a perfect example of *eisegesis*. Here was a businessman bent on finding a business ethic in the New Testament. So that's the folly of *eisegesis*.

3

Developing a Christian Mind in a Non-Christian Society

With scripture's authority now clearer in our thinking, and having covered the basics of interpretation, I want us to turn towards the application of biblical truth to our society. So let's work to explore a Christian way of thinking, and how to develop a Christian lens on the world.

I have divided the subject into three sections: the importance of the mind in general, developing a Christian mind in particular, and the foundations of Christian thinking.

Consider two friends, Maria and Jon, who bump into each other in the supermarket. Maria has a preoccupied expression.

Jon asks: 'What's the matter with you? You look worried!'
Maria responds: 'Oh, I am. I keep thinking about
the world's situation.'
Jon has a solution: Well, you ought to take things
more philosophically. Stop thinking!'

It is a rather delightful idea that the way to become more philosophical is to do less thinking. But those two friends have given birth to the twins called Mindlessness and Meaninglessness. The apostle Paul urged that the Corinthians 'Stop thinking' (1 Corinthians 14:20). But his exhortation was very different from Jon's. What Paul says is: Stop thinking like babies. Yes, be childish in the area of malice, and ignorant of evil. But in your thinking, you must grow up and become mature!

I. The Importance of the Mind in General

I want to suggest three beneficial results of a proper use of our mind.

a) It glorifies our creator. We believe that God has made us rational beings in his own image and likeness and that he's given us, in nature and in scripture, a double, rational revelation of himself. Indeed it was Sir Francis Bacon, a lawyer and a leader in Britain in the 16th and 17th centuries,[16] who said that God has given us two books – and not one only. There is the book of his words, which we call scripture, and the book of his works, which we call nature. So nature study and Bible study can go hand in hand. They can belong to one another because both of them are revelations of God. So in our Bible study and in our nature study we can, as Johann Kepler[17] said, be thinking God's thoughts after him. A proper use of the mind in this way glorifies our creator.

b) It enriches our Christian life. Let me give three brief examples: Worship, faith and guidance.

The best biblical definition of worship that I know is Psalm 105, namely 'to glory in God's holy name'. But you can't glory in God's holy name if you don't know his name or the kind of person he is. We have to know his name before we can glory in his name. So the use of the mind is essential in worship.

Christians often see faith and reason as set over against each other; but this is never so in scripture. Faith and *sight* are contrasted, but not faith and reason, for faith is a reasoning trust. The Psalmist says: 'Those who know your name put their trust in you.'[18] Faith rests on knowledge. The more we reflect on God's nature and his covenant and his promises, the more faith arises within us. So faith rests on reason.

The Psalmist gives us a threefold promise of divine guidance in Psalm 3:8. God says: I will guide you, I will instruct you in the way you should go, I will lead you with my eyes upon you. But then verse 9 qualifies those promises: 'But don't be like a horse or mule that has no understanding, whose mouth needs to be held with bit and bridle or it will not stay near you.' So God will guide, but not if we behave like horses and mules. Why not? For the elementary reason that you are not a horse or a mule! So don't expect God to behave towards you as if you were. So we have the promise and the prohibition – a beautiful example of biblical balance. A proper use of the mind enriches our Christian discipleship.

Faith and sight are contrasted, but not faith and reason

c) **It strengthens our evangelistic witness.** In the Book of Acts, the record of the ministry of the apostles of Jesus, evangelism (the proclamation of the gospel) and apologetics (the defence of the gospel) went together. So Paul could describe his whole ministry in the three words: 'We persuade people'. You can't persuade people if you don't use arguments. And you can't use arguments if you don't use your mind. Of course, Paul knew very well that he had to trust in the Holy Spirit – only the Holy Spirit can lead people to faith in Jesus. But the Holy Spirit is a spirit of truth so he leads people to faith in Jesus. It is he who opens our mind to attend to the evidence.

2. Developing a Christian Mind

What is a Christian mind? Let's clarify what it is not. A Christian mind is not a mind that is thinking about specifically Christian or religious topics. Rather, a Christian mind is one which thinks about even the most secular topics from a Christian perspective. A Christian mind is not a mind that is preoccupied with churches and chapels and hymn books and prayer books and Bibles and bishops. A Christian mind is a mind that is seeking the will of God in relation to our home, job, community, discipleship, politics, economics, north-south economic inequality, unemployment, human rights, the natural environment and every other issue which pertains to our lives and our world. However 'secular' our topic may be, we are to think about it Christianly, from a Christian point of view.

The person who gave currency to the phrase 'a Christian mind' was Harry Blamires, in a book titled *The Christian Mind* published in 1963.[19] These years later, it is still worth reading. The best way to grasp the meaning of a Christian mind is to see it operating within the framework of biblical history. The Bible thinks of history not so much in terms of the rise and fall of dynasties and empires and civilizations as secular history books do, but in terms of four great events of history – past, present and future, and the four epochs which they introduce. Namely the Creation of the world, the Fall of humankind, the Redemption achieved through the Cross, and the Consummation at the end of time.

The Bible thinks of history in terms of four great events and the epochs they introduce

Epoch 1: The Creation of the world. Essential to the Christian mind is the conviction that God made everything out of an original Nothing. That is to say: When he began the creative process, nothing existed except himself. Only God is eternal. Whatever may have been the mode and the time of creation, the climax is clear. The climax of the creative process was mankind, male and female, made in God's image and likeness. To us human beings, God entrusted stewardship over the environment; he endowed us with rational, moral, social and spiritual faculties which distinguish us from the animal creation, and above all, he created us with the capacity to love, finding fulfilment in him, in each other and in our work. And God pronounced everything that he had made to be good.

Epoch 2: The Fall of humankind. Adam and Eve, created for loving fellowship in God, listened to the lies of Satan instead of to the truth of God, and rebelled against his authority. In consequence, all their relationships became skewed – their relationship to each other in blaming each other, their relationship to the good earth, which was cursed because of them, and their relation especially to God who banished them from the Garden. That's the supreme tragedy of the human condition, and I'd like us to think clearly about this. The supreme tragedy of the human condition today is that human beings who were made by God, like God, and for God, should now be living without God. And all our senses of alienation and loneliness and disorientation are due to the disruption of these relationships.

That's the supreme tragedy of the human condition

Epoch 3: The Redemption achieved on the Cross. God could quite justly have abandoned or destroyed the human race. Instead, in his love, he planned our redemption. He promised that the seed of the woman would crush the serpent's head. He called Abraham and promised to bless him and to bless all the families of the earth. The Old Testament is the outworking of this meta-narrative, or, if you like, mega-narrative. These foundational promises are of immense importance. And then in the fullness of time, Christ came – the seed of the woman, the seed of Abraham and the seed of David. Christ lived a perfect life of love. He had no sin of his own for which atonement needed to be made, but on the cross he took our place, he bore our sin and he died our death. And then God raised him from the dead and exalted him in order to vindicate his redeeming work. Ever since then it has been possible for human beings like us to experience a new birth or a new creation. So we read in 2 Corinthians 5: 17: 'If anybody is in Christ *kaine ktisis*' (new creation). There is no verb in that verse. It is a stark and simple fact of all who are in Christ, or united with Christ. All things have become new.

Epoch 4: The Consummation. *Already* the kingdom of God has broken into human history but *not yet* has it come in its fullness. So far, we have only tasted the power of the age to come, and the banquet is still in the future. But the Lord Jesus Christ is going to come back in sheer magnificence, in power and glory – to create a new heaven and a new earth to consummate all things.

Meanwhile, we are living in between-times: between kingdom come and kingdom coming; between kingdom inaugurated and kingdom consummated; between he *already* and the *not yet*.

This might be called the Christian meta-narrative. It's the frame which God himself has given us: a fourfold grid through which to filter all our Christian thinking, as we shall see in the next sections.

3. Foundations of Christian Thinking

The reality of God on the one hand, and the paradox of our humanness on the other – created in God's image, yet fallen – are the two foundation stones of all our thinking.

The Christian mind acknowledges God as the supreme and ultimate reality behind and beyond all phenomena, as Creator, Sustainer, Lord, Father, Judge. The Christian mind is a *godly* mind, and it could never call people good if they are ungodly, for the biblical view of goodness is godliness.[20] A Christian mind affirms that the first and great commandment is to love the Lord our God. And only the second commandment is to love our neighbour.

So if we believe in the reality of God, in God-centredness, there are two corollaries which arise. The first is the meaning of wisdom and the second is the pre-eminence of humility. I guess we'd all like to be thought wise. Wisdom is a prominent theme in the Bible. In addition to the law and the prophets, there is the wisdom literature – Job, Psalms, Proverbs, Ecclesiastes and the Song of Solomon. Just for fun, let me share with you, in case you don't know it, that little doggerel that goes:

King David and King Solomon lived many, many lives,
had many, many concubines and many, many wives.
But when old age o'ertook them, with many, many qualms,
King Solomon wrote the Proverbs, and King David
wrote the Psalms.

The wisdom books are concerned with what we call *meaning*: What it *means* to be a human being, and how suffering and evil and injustice and love fit in with this meaning. Think of Ecclesiastes. This book is best known for its pessimistic refrain: 'Vanity of vanities, all is vanity'. Or, as the New International Version translates it, 'Meaningless! Meaningless! ... Utterly meaningless!'. So Ecclesiastes demonstrates the futility, or meaninglessness, of a life that is lived without God. The writer demonstrates the futility of the human life which is imprisoned in time and space and ignores the reality of God. So if reality is restricted to time – the brief human life span with all its injustice and pain – beginning with birth and ending, like the animals, in death, then indeed: Vanity of vanities, all is vanity.

Ecclesiastes demonstrates the futility of life without God

If reality is restricted not only to time but to space, to the human experience under the sun with no ultimate reference point above the sun, then again, all is: 'Meaningless! Meaningless! ... Utterly meaningless!' Everything is futile and 'a chasing after the wind'. Only God can give meaning to life because only he can supply the missing dimension. God adds eternity to time, and God adds transcendence to space. And that's why several times in the wisdom literature, we read 'the fear of the Lord is the beginning of wisdom'. Wisdom begins with an acknowledgement of the reality of God. Hence the tragedy of the spiritual vacuum in so many lives, and the hostility to the Christian mind of a secularism which denies the reality of God.

Let me give you an example from Theodore Roszak.[21] His interesting book *Where the Wasteland Ends: Politics and Transcendence in Post-industrial Society* is an exposure of western materialism and its emptiness. Roszak laments what he calls delightfully a 'coca-colonisation' of the world. We're suffering, he says, from a psychic claustrophobia within a scientific worldview in which the human spirit cannot breathe. He attacks science, by which I'm sure he meant pseudo-science, for its reductionist assault on human life, its debunking spirit, its arrogant claim to be able to explain everything, and its undoing of the mysteries. As far as I know, he was not a Christian, but he was aware that pseudo-science un-does the mysteries and allows us no mysteries any more. He goes on: 'What science can measure is only a portion of what man can know. This materialistic world of objective science is not nearly spacious enough for us.' And then with this remarkable phrase he concludes: 'Without transcendence a person shrivels.'

So here is a powerful call for transcendence from a non-Christian writer, realising that human beings need more than the material.

The pre-eminence of humility. Because the Christian mind is a godly mind, it exalts the virtue of humility; it is a humble mind. Because of the God-centredness of the Bible, nothing is so obscene as human pride, and nothing is so attractive as humility. I think of Nebuchadnezzar, the Emperor of Babylon who was strutting like a peacock on the flat roof of his palace, and as he talked to himself he said: 'Is not this great Babylon which I have built by the might of my power, and for the glory of my kingdom...' (Daniel 4:30) Have you ever noticed that he claimed for himself the power and the kingdom and the glory? It's the exact opposite of the doxology. We are to say: '*Yours* is the kingdom and the power and the glory!'

Nothing is so obscene as pride, nothing so attractive as humility

But Nebuchadnezzar said: 'They're *mine*. They're *not yours*.' So it's not surprising that while the words were still on his lips, God's judgement fell upon him. He was deprived of his kingdom and driven from his palace. He lived with animals and ate like them; his body became wet with dew, his hair grew long like eagle's feathers, his nails grew like claws. In other words, he went mad. And it was only when he acknowledged that the most high God rules in the kingdoms of man, and he lifted his eyes in humble worship to God, that his sanity and his kingdom were *simultaneously* restored to him – because pride and madness go together, as do humility and reason.

Now let's come to the Lord Jesus and think especially on his example and on his teaching. We all know from Philippians 2 that, although sharing the very essence of God, he did not regard equality with God a privilege to be selfishly enjoyed, but emptied himself of his glory and humbled himself to serve. He became obedient to death, even death on the cross. Humility is the essence of the Son of God. Several times during his public ministry, he took a little child, put him in the midst, and told his hearers that if you want to be great, you have got to humble yourself like a little child.

At no point does the Christian mind come into more violent collision with a secular mind than in its insistence upon humility. The wisdom of the world despises humility. Even the ethnic religions do not specifically commend it, and Western culture has imbibed more than it realises of the power philosophy of Nietzsche, who dreamed of the emergence of a ruler race: tough, rash, masculine and overbearing. The ideal of Nietzsche was the *Übermensch*, the superhuman – but the ideal of Jesus was the little child. And there is no possibility of compromise between those two images – we have to choose. Thus the reality of God as Creator, Sustainer, Lord, Saviour, Father, Judge is the first foundation stone on which all our Christian thinking must be based. The Christian mind refuses to honour anything which dishonours God. It learns to evaluate everything according to whether it gives glory to God or withholds glory from God. Hence wisdom is the fear of God, and humility is the pre-eminent virtue. So that's our first foundation stone: the reality of God and its corollaries.

The wisdom of the world despises humility

The paradox of our humanness. In answer to its own question: What is man? (What does it mean to be a human being?), the Bible affirms both the Creation and the Fall.

That's two of the four epochs we thought about earlier. The Bible affirms both the glory and the shame of our human condition, both our unique dignity as creatures made in the image of God, and our equally unique depravity as sinners under the judgement of God. And the Christian critique of much of modern philosophy and ideology is that it's either too naive in its optimism or too negative in its pessimism. We need the Bible to retain the balance.

Humanists tend to be very optimistic. They believe that human beings are nothing but the product of a blind evolutionary process. But at the same time they have boundless confidence in the future evolutionary potential (as they believe it to be) of the human race. One day, humanists say, we shall be able to control our own destiny. But this kind of optimism takes no account of that twist of self-centredness which theologians call original sin, and which spoils and frustrates the plans of all social reformers.

Human beings are a strange, bewildering paradox

At the other extreme are the existentialists who reach not only into pessimism, but even despair. Because there is no God, they say, there are no values any longer, so nothing has meaning, everything is absurd. As Mark Twain, the great American wit, once said: 'If man could be crossed with a cat, it would improve man and deteriorate the cat.' I think you'll agree it's a little bit pessimistic – in fact, too pessimistic – it doesn't take into account the love, the joy, the heroism, the self-sacrifice which have adorned the human story.

So we leave behind us both the optimism and the pessimism of alternative ideologies, and come to biblical Christians as the third group, who avoid both the extremes we've considered. As J S Whale[22] of Cambridge University once said: 'What we need is neither the easy optimism of the humanist nor the dark pessimism of the cynic, but the radical realism of the Bible.'

So what is this radical realism of the Bible? According to the Bible, human beings are created in the image of God, and the image has been distorted, though not destroyed. Human beings are, in fact, a strange, bewildering paradox, capable both of the loftiest nobility and of the basest cruelty.

We are able to behave at one moment like God in whose image we have been made, and at the next moment like the beast from which we were meant to be forever distinct. Human beings are able to think, to choose, to create, to love and to worship. But we are also able to covet, to fight, to hate, to take revenge and to kill. Human beings are the inventors of hospitals for the care of the sick, universities for the acquisition of wisdom and, in addition, churches for the worship of God. But human beings are also the inventors of torture chambers, concentration camps and nuclear arsenals.

So, as the Christian mind reflects on the situation around us, it will never forget the paradox of our humanness: that we are both noble and ignoble, both moral and immoral, both wise and foolish, both godlike and bestial. Let me share part of a quote I fell upon, which captures so much, so eloquently: 'I am dust and ashes, perverse and wayward, beset with needs, the quintessence of dust, and to dust I shall return. But there is something else in me: Dust I may be, but troubled dust; dust that breathes, dust that has strange premonitions of a glory in store, an inheritance that will one day be my own. So my life is stretched out in a painful dialectic between ashes and transfiguration. I'm a riddle unto myself, and I'm an exasperating enigma.' This strange duality of dust and glory – that's the paradox.

'I'm a riddle... an exasperating enigma'

Let me give you two examples of this paradox.

We all know the importance for our own mental health of understanding who we are, and having an accurate self-image. Some have a very exaggerated image and become conceited. Others have too low an image and struggle with crippling inferiority feelings. But the Christian way is to remember the paradox of our humanness, and to acknowledge that we are the product both of our Creation in the image of God and the Fall with its consequent sinfulness. Then we shall be able both to affirm our true self (what we are by Creation) and to deny our false self (what we are by the Fall), which is wayward, self-centred and aggressive. I don't think it is right for us to talk about loving ourselves, but we can affirm everything in us that comes from the Creation, and then, as Jesus taught his disciples, deny everything about ourselves that is traceable to the Fall.

My second example brings us into the sphere of politics. Do you know the difference between capitalism and socialism? In capitalism man exploits man but in socialism it's the other way around. Democracy, I think all of us will agree, is the safest form of government which has yet been invented – because it reflects the paradox of our humanness. On the one hand, it takes Creation seriously because a government is dependent on consent, and ongoing government dependent on representation, at least in theory. It gives us a share in the decision making process, and it treats us as responsible adults. That is because of what we are by the Creation. But on the other hand it takes the Fall seriously, and it refuses to concentrate power in the hands of a few because it knows that it's not safe to do so. So it disperses power. Indeed, the dispersal of power is the very essence of democracy. And thus it protects us from our own folly. Some of you will know the name of a New York theological ethicist, Reinhold Niebuhr.[23] His famous epigram is this: Man's capacity for justice makes democracy possible, and man's inclination to injustice makes democracy necessary.

So how can we develop a Christian mind? There is no slick or easy way to do so but only the sweat of study, and especially what I like to call the discipline of 'double listening'. This discipline is in the first place to listen to the word of God, to become profound Bible students and scholars, not to read it superficially but to go on reading until, as Spurgeon[24] puts it, our very blood becomes 'bibline', and we absorb the teaching of scripture. But we must not only listen to the word of God, for we need to listen secondly to the voices of the modern world - its cries of pain, its shouts of anger, its sighs and groans of alienation.

Now, of course, we don't listen to the voices of the modern world with the same respect with which we listen to the word of God. We listen to the word of God in order to believe and obey it. We listen to the voices of the modern world in order to understand them. We cannot apply the word to the world unless we do this double listening with faithfulness and with sensitivity.

A mind and a heart

Now let me add briefly a note of caution. I often say to our students at the London Institute[25] that we are not in the business of breeding tadpoles. Picture them now in your mind's eye: these aquatic larvae of frogs and toads, each with a huge head and nothing much else besides. I know some Christian tadpoles whose heads are crammed with biblical theology, but that's all there is about them. As well as a Christian mind, we also need a Christian heart. We need to be growing as whole Christian people, for whom everything about us is submitted to the lordship of Jesus Christ. Let's relate this to the area of social responsibility, as we learn both to think clearly about the world, and to feel deeply. The Lord Jesus Christ himself was moved to indignation in the face of evil, and moved to compassion towards its victims. He wept and he groaned, we are told in John 11.

You may know the novel *The Chosen* by Chaim Potok, a well-known Jewish novelist, or you may have seen the movie. Let me tell you the story very briefly. *The Chosen* is about two youths in New York City during and after the Second World War. One is Danny whose father is a rabbi, Rabbi Saunders, and the other is Reuven. In these men, the two very different Jewish traditions come into collision with one another as the story progresses. The point is this: Rabbi Saunders never speaks to his son Danny throughout the novel or throughout the movie. He brings him up in silence and never speaks to him, except when he is teaching him out of the Talmud, and we wonder why it is.

I know some Christian tadpoles whose heads are crammed with biblical theology

It's not until the end that the mystery is explained. Rabbi Saunders says that God had blessed him with a brilliant son, a boy with a mind like a jewel, and you think he would be proud of that. But when young Danny was only four years old, his father saw him reading a book, and was frightened because of Danny's response to it. Now you think the father would be proud of a boy who could read at that age. The book was about the suffering of a deported Jew, and Danny had no sense or feeling for the sufferings of this poor man, he simply enjoyed the book.

So Rabbi Saunders cried to God: 'What have you done to me? There is only his mind. He is a mind in a body without a soul.' He again cried to God and said: 'What have you done to me? A mind like this! I need my son to have a heart, a soul. I need my son to have compassion, mercy, strength to suffer, not a mind without a heart!' And so Rabbi Saunders followed an ancient Hasidic tradition and brought the boy up in silence, so that 'in the silence between us', he said, 'Danny began to hear the world crying.'

In the final scene of reconciliation between the father and the son, the rabbi says that Danny had to learn through the wisdom of the pain of silence that a mind without a heart is nothing. So, dear sisters and brothers, we need a Christian mind. But we also need a heart if we are to be a whole Christian person. May God give us both.

4

Making a Christian Impact in Today's World

We're going to consider one of the most important questions facing Christians in every age and in every place. And that is: what values and standards are going to dominate our national culture?

Most countries are increasingly pluralistic both in race and in religion. So Christianity, Islam, secularism, materialism, ancient religions and modern cults are all competing for the soul of the country.

Now for Christians, this is first and foremost an evangelistic question. Will Jesus Christ be given the honour that is due to his name? God has highly exalted him, given him the name above every name, that at the name of Jesus every knee shall bow and every tongue confess that he is Lord. God has super-exalted the Lord Jesus with every knee bowing to him. But if it is an evangelistic question, it is also a social and cultural question. Will Christians be able to influence their country so that the values and standards of the kingdom of God permeate the whole national culture?

What do we mean by the 'national culture'? Its consensus on moral questions, its equal regard for men, women and children, its attitude towards marriage and the family, its perspective on the sanctity of human life including the unborn, the handicapped and the senile, its administration of justice and its conduct of business, its academic research, the education of its youth, its recognition of human rights especially of ethnic minorities, its concern for the homeless and the unemployed and people who are trapped in the cycle of poverty, its attitude to dissidents, its treatment of criminals, its stewardship of the natural environment, its use of power and the whole way of life of its citizens. That's a long list, and all this and more constitutes the national culture, that is the values and standards which are recognized as acceptable.

What do we mean by the 'national culture'?

There can be no doubt that Jesus wants his values and standards to prevail. He loves righteousness, and he hates inequity. So he sends his people out into the world not only to preach the gospel and make disciples but also to sweeten the whole community and make it more pleasing to God – more just, more participatory and more free. Now these are mega-claims, and the question before us now is: What is the justification for them? Is there a biblical basis for this? And if so – what is it? As you can imagine, it contains the well-known metaphors or models of salt and light. Let's have a look at Matthew 5:13-16. Jesus said in the Sermon on the Mount:

You are the salt of the earth. But if the salt loses its saltiness, how can it be made salty again? It's no longer good for anything except to be thrown out and be trampled by men. You are the light of the world. A city on a hill cannot be hidden, neither do people light a lamp and put it under a bowl. Instead, they put it on a stand, and it gives light to everyone in the house. In the same way let your light shine before men so that they may see your good deeds and praise your Father in heaven.

We are all very familiar with salt and light. They are two of the commonest household commodities. They are to be found in virtually every home in the world. Certainly, everybody used them in the Palestine of Jesus' day. He will have known them from his boyhood. He must often have watched his mother Mary use salt in the kitchen. In those days before refrigeration had been invented, salt was used not so much for flavouring as for preservative and antiseptic purposes. So Mary will have put salt onto the fish, and she will have rubbed it onto the meat or she will have left meat or fish to soak in salty water. And then she will have lit the simple oil lamps when the sun went down.

So these are the images that Jesus chose to indicate the impact or the influence which he intended his people to exert in the world. The question before us as thoughtful and intelligent people is: What did Jesus mean? What is it legitimate for us to deduce from his deliberate choice of metaphor. What did he mean by being salt and light to society? I believe that by the models of salt and light, Jesus is teaching us four truths. Please weigh them for yourself.

I. Christians are radically different from non-Christians

Christians should live in a radically-different way from others. Both images, salt and light, set the two communities in contrast to one another. There is the world which, with all its evil and tragedy, is like a dark night. And *you* are to be the dark world's light. So you and the world are set over against each other in antithesis. There is the world, like rotting meat and decaying fish. And *you* are to be the salt, hindering social decay. We may say in a modern English idiom, the two are as different as chalk and cheese, or as oil and water. In the idiom of the day, Jesus expressed this radical difference as that between light and darkness and salt and decay.

This, friends, is a major theme of the whole Bible. God is calling out a people for himself. And this people is to be his special people. Their vocation is to be different from the world around them, from the prevailing culture. 'Be holy!' he says to them, to us, 'For I, the Lord, your God, am holy.'

So there's a clear call to be different

I want to give you an example from each of the law, the gospels and the epistles. We read in Leviticus 18:1,2 as God speaks through Moses to his people: 'You must not do as they do in the land of Egypt where you used to live. And you must not do as they do in the land of Canaan into which I am bringing you. You must not follow their standards, you must obey my precepts.' So there's a clear call to be different.

Then if we move on into the gospels, in the Sermon on the Mount in Matthew 6 Jesus says: 'Do not be like them.' There are the pagans, the Pharisees, the hypocrites – 'do not be like them.' As simple as that – monosyllables. And then we move on to the epistles, the well-known Romans 12:1-2: 'Do not be conformed to the fashions around you.'

II. Christians must penetrate and permeate non-Christian society

We are to be morally and spiritually distinct, as we've seen, but we are not to be socially segregated. On the contrary: 'Let your light shine!' In other words: Let it permeate, let it penetrate the darkness! Don't light your lamp and put it under your bed or under a bucket, and don't hide it away in some dark cupboard – put your lamp on a lampstand and let its light shine out into the darkness. In other words: Let the good news of Jesus Christ, who is the light of the world, spread throughout society by your words and by your deeds.

This is equally true of the salt. The salt must penetrate the meat. A lamp does no good if it's stowed in a cupboard, the salt does no good if it stays in the cellar or in the saltshaker. The light must shine into the darkness, the salt must soak into the meat. Both models illustrate the same thing: the process of penetration of society. The light of the world, the salt of the earth.

So what does it mean to permeate society? Forgive another British illustration. You may have heard of the Fabian Society, founded in 1884 by George Bernard Shaw the dramatist and others. Its purpose was to make Britain socialist – not by a Bolshevik revolution, nor by intrigue and conspiracy, but by a policy of infiltration. They wanted to permeate the Conservative and Liberal Parties. In the 1880s there was no Labour Party, no socialist party in Britain. So their desire was to permeate the Conservative and Liberal Parties with socialist ideas and ideals. And then, somewhat later, H G Wells quarrelled with the founding fathers and pronounced their policy a failure. As H G Wells said: 'They permeate English society with their reputed socialism about as much or as little as a mouse may be said to permeate a cat.' Instead of permeating it, they had been swallowed by it. And Christians are often swallowed up by the prevailing culture. Too many of us hide away in our dark little cupboards or we stay snug in our elegant little salt cellars.

We desperately need Christians in the secular professions, media, and the public arenas

Let me illustrate this further. As a young man, I was led to believe in a pyramid of vocations. I was told that if I was out and out for Jesus Christ, I would become a cross-cultural missionary – these were our heroes and heroines, at the top of the pyramid. Then I was told that if I was not as keen for Jesus as that, I would stay at home and become a pastor. And if I wasn't as keen as that, I would no doubt become a doctor or a teacher. But if I became a politician or went into the mass media of communication, I was not far from backsliding. That's what I was taught.

I've long ago had to blow up the pyramid and expose this myth because we desperately need Christians in the secular professions, in the media, in the public arenas. Through more and more Christians who are thoughtfully applying biblical truth in the workplace, we can permeate society.

III. Christians can influence and change Non-Christian society

I dare to say this, although not everybody agrees, because salt and light are both powerfully-effective commodities. They change the environment into which they are introduced. So when salt is introduced into meat and fish, something *happens*: Bacterial decay is hindered. And when the light is switched on, something happens: the darkness is dispelled. Further, salt and light have complementary effects. The influence of salt is largely negative: it hinders bacterial decay. The influence of light is positive: It illumines the darkness. Just so, the influence of Christians is intended by Jesus to be both negative – hindering the spread of evil – and positive – promoting the spread of truth and goodness, and especially of the gospel of Christ.

So why don't we Christians have a more wholesome effect on society? When we look at the deteriorating trends around us, we see social injustice, racial conflict, unemployment, poverty, violence on the streets, corruption in high places, sexual promiscuity, the scourge of HIV and AIDS, the disregard of the sanctity of human life, and so we may go on.

Why don't Christians have more effect on society?

Who is to blame for these things? Well, we are likely to blame everybody except ourselves. And certainly people are responsible for their own conduct. But if the house is dark at night, there is no sense in blaming the house for its darkness. That's what happens when the sun goes down. The question is: Where is the light? Similarly, if the meat goes bad and becomes inedible, there is no sense in blaming the meat for its decay. That's what happens when the bacteria are left free to breed. The question is: Where is the salt? And just so if society becomes corrupt like a dark night or stinking fish, there is no sense in blaming society for its corruption. That's what happens when human evil is unchecked and unrestrained. The question is: Where is the church? Where is the salt and where is the light of Jesus? It's hypocritical to raise our eyebrows and shrug our shoulders as if we were not in any way responsible.

Jesus told us to be the salt and the light of society. If darkness and rottenness abound, it is to a large extent our fault because we are not acting as salt and light as we should do. We must accept much of the blame. We must also accept with fresh determination the role which Jesus has assigned to us, namely to be salt and light to society. It is not only individuals who can be changed. Societies can also be changed.

We cannot perfect society. We are not being guilty of the old-fashioned social gospel. But we can improve it. Christians are not utopians. Not until Christ comes in glory will there be a perfect society of peace and justice. But meanwhile, until that day, history is full of examples of social improvement: rising standards of health and hygiene, greater availability of literacy and education, the emancipation of women, better conditions in mines, factories and prisons, the abolition of slavery and the slave trade – all these things are to some degree attributable to the influence of the followers of Jesus. We cannot claim responsibility for them all, but we can claim that through his followers, Jesus has had an enormous influence for good.

We cannot perfect society, but we can improve it

You may know the name of Professor K S Latourette of Yale University, an expert in social ethics and mission. He wrote a seven-volume work on the history of the expansion of Christianity, and I quote from the very end of these seven volumes: 'No life ever lived on this planet has been so influential in the affairs of men and nations as the life of Christ. From that brief life, and its apparent frustration, has flowed a more powerful force for the triumphal waging of man's long battle than any other influence in the world.'

So how does social change take place? I want to suggest that Christians have six weapons in their armoury:

1. Prayer

I beg you not to dismiss this as a pious platitude. We Christians believe that God hears and answers prayer. So the apostle commands us as a priority to pray for our national leaders so that we may 'lead a quiet and peaceful life in all godliness'. Yet, when

I visit some churches, there is almost no serious intercession. I sometimes wonder whether the low progress in, say, social change is due more than anything else to the prayerlessness of the people of God. Some years ago, President Marcos of the Philippines was removed from power. And Filipino Christians attributed this not to people power but to prayer power. So we should take the task of public intercession much more seriously. Supposing in public worship in our churches, we were to bow down before the living God for five, ten, fifteen minutes, or half an hour? I wonder what God might be free to do if his people pray. That's our first weapon.

2. Evangelism

Evangelism has an indispensable part to play in social change. For Christians, social responsibility depends on socially-responsible Christians, and socially-responsible Christians are the fruit of evangelism. It's when the Holy Spirit changes us that we begin to develop a social conscience, and we gain the vision and the courage to change our society. Evangelism and social responsibility go together. They've been said to be like two wings of a bird and two blades of a pair of scissors.

3. Example

Human beings are imitative by nature. So there is great power in example. One individual Christian who takes an uncompromising stand for righteousness encourages others to follow. One Christian home and family can influence a whole neighbourhood. A dedicated Christian group in school or university, in hospital, or in the factory or the office can change its atmosphere and its accepted values. And the local church is meant by God to be what is called a sign of the kingdom – a model of what human community looks like when it comes under the rule of God – and is an attractive alternative society.

4. Argument

In the end, unjust social structures can be changed only by legislation. Legislation cannot make bad people good but it can reduce the level of evil in society and it can make it more pleasing to God. Let me quote from the great civil rights activist Martin Luther King: 'Morality cannot be legislated but behaviour can be regulated. Judicial laws may not change the heart but they can restrain the heartless. The law cannot make an employer love me, but it can keep him from refusing to hire me on account of the colour of my skin.' I think that is well said. Yet, in a democracy legislation depends on consent, consent depends on consensus (that is, on public opinion), and consensus depends on argument and, indeed, on winning the argument.

5. Socio-political action

There are two possible definitions of politics. One is narrow, and the other is broad. The narrow definition is that politics is the science of government, it's the framing of laws which embody the beliefs and values of society. The broader definition is from polis, the Greek word for a city, seeing politics as the art of living together in a community. By the narrow sense, politics is for the politicians. It is not the function, for example, of pastors, to develop political programmes for legislative change. In the broad sense, however, politics is for everybody – since all of us are called to be responsible citizens in the community. Jesus sends us all into the world to serve him. Politicians could never succeed, and their policies could never become law without a groundswell of public support from the constituencies. So we have a responsibility to be conscientious citizens and to exercise our democratic rights – to vote and seek to influence other people's votes, to speak up and to write on issues of social ethics, and to engage in public peaceful protest and witness; and in these ways to be salt and light to the community.

6. Suffering

It sounds strange to call this a weapon. I mean by this a willingness to suffer for what we believe in. Willingness to suffer is really a test of our authenticity. Have you ever thought of evangelism and social action as very costly activities? For both the gospel of Christ and the moral standards of Christ are unpopular. They challenge the selfishness of the human heart. They challenge our self-indulgence. So those who defend God's law and those who defend God's gospel, are bound to suffer for it.

Each of these six is a powerful weapon in its own right, and together this is a formidable Christian armoury at our disposal. Don't let's underestimate the influence which even a Christian minority is able to exert. You may have heard of Robert Bellah, Professor of Sociology at the University of California in Berkeley.[26] As a Christian himself, he was concerned that Christians should be active in their society. I want to quote an extraordinary statement that he made when being interviewed by the magazine Psychology Today. He said: 'I think we should not underestimate the significance of a small group of people who have a new vision of a just and gentle world... The quality of a culture may be changed when two per cent of its people have a new vision.' We are in most cases many more than two per cent. We could have more influence than we realise.

IV. Christians must retain their Christian distinctives

Salt must retain its saltiness, otherwise it becomes useless. You can't even throw it on the compost heap. And similarly, light must retain its brightness, otherwise it will never dispel the darkness. Just so, we Christians, if we are to have any influence on society, must not only penetrate society but refuse to conform to it or assimilate it. We must retain our Christian convictions, our Christian standards, our Christian values, our Christian lifestyle. And we must retain these standards of the kingdom of God. So naturally, you ask: What are our Christian distinctives? What is the salt which is to soak into the meat? What is the light which is to shine into the darkness? Answer: The Sermon on the Mount will tell us. For in the Sermon on the Mount, Jesus describes the citizens of the Kingdom of God, the members of his new society. And I select from the rest of the Sermon on the Mount three distinctives.

a) **Christ calls us to a greater righteousness.** We read in Matthew 5:20: 'Unless your righteousness exceeds the righteousness of the Scribes and Pharisees, you will not even enter into the Kingdom of God.' Now the disciples of Jesus, when they heard it, must have been utterly dumbfounded. The Scribes and the Pharisees were the most righteous people on earth. They calculated, as you may know, that the Law contained 248 commandments and 365 prohibitions, making 613 rules and regulations altogether. And Jesus says that unless we are *more* righteous than the most righteous people on earth, we'll never even enter the Kingdom! 'Has the master lost his reason? Or what can he mean?' they must have thought.

The explanation is easy: The Christian righteousness is greater than Pharisean righteousness because it's deeper – it is a righteousness of the heart, not just of words and deeds. For example: 'The law says "You shall not kill", but I say to you that you shall not even be angry. Again, the law says "You shall not commit adultery", but I say to you that if you look at a woman to lust after her, you have committed adultery with her in your heart.' Christian righteousness is heart righteousness.

That's why it necessitates a new heart and a new birth. So Christ calls us to a deeper righteousness, which is greater than that of the Pharisees.

b) Christ calls us to a wider love. Look at Matthew 5:43: 'You have heard that it was said by the men of old "You shall love your neighbour and hate your enemy."' Let's pause a moment. That is a scandalous misquotation of the Old Testament. The law said: You shall love your neighbour as yourself.' It was the Pharisees who seem to have indulged in moral casuistry, asking themselves, 'Who is my neighbour that I have to love? In reply to themselves, they said 'Why did I not think of it before? My neighbour is my co-religionist, my neighbour is my fellow Jew. So if it's only my neighbour that I have to love, it's tantamount to saying that I can hate my enemy.' Jesus responds that our neighbour, in the vocabulary of God, includes our enemy! (v44). 'I say to you: Love your enemy, pray for those who persecute you, do good to those who hate you and *then* you will be the children of your heavenly Father. For he makes his sun to rise on the evil and on the good, and he sends rain on the just and on the unjust.'

That is a scandalous misquotation of the Old Testament

God's love is all-embracing. So ours must be too. If we love only those who love us, we are no better than unbelievers. Unbelievers love those who love them. Parents love their children, for this is the natural love. But, brothers and sisters, Christ calls us to a supernatural love. If we want to be authentic children of our heavenly Father, we must love our enemies as he, Jesus, has done. And our enemy is the one who is after us with a knife or with a gun or who wants to take away something precious like our good name, our reputation. Christ calls us to a wider love – not just for our family and our friends, but for our enemies as well.

c) **Christ calls us to a nobler ambition.** All human beings are ambitious. Ambition is simply the desire to succeed. And our ambition in the words of Jesus is what we seek, what we set our hearts on as the supreme good to which we devote our lives. And what is that? Well in the end, Jesus teaches in Matthew 6, that there are only two options before us. One (v32) is to be concerned mainly about ourselves and our material comfort: what shall we eat, what shall we drink, what shall we wear. The alternative (v33) is to: Seek first the Kingdom of God and his righteousness, and then all these things will be added to you as well. So to be preoccupied with ourselves and our bodies – food, drink and clothing – is a hopelessly inadequate ambition for the children of God.

As Jesus taught in the Lord's Prayer: The very first thing we must pray for is not our daily bread, the forgiveness of our sins, the deliverance from evil. It is the name of God and the kingdom of God and the will of God. And then, if we are really taken up by a desire for his name, his kingdom, his will, we can say: Heavenly Father, by the way, you won't forget, will you, that there is also my daily bread etc. So we need to get the priorities right as Christ calls us to a nobler ambition.

Only then will our salt retain its saltiness and our light retain its brightness, so we can rub salt and shine light into the world and into human society.

In conclusion I call you, as I call myself, to a double repentance. We need first and foremost to repent of our compromises. Jesus sets before us in antithesis to one another his way and the way of the world – the narrow path and the broad road that leads to destruction. And he compels us to choose. So let's turn from our half-heartedness. Let's give up our little prudential compromises, and let's make Jesus Christ the supreme Lord of every part of our lives.

And if we are to repent of our compromise, we are also to repent of our pessimism. If Christian hypocrisy is horrid, Christian pessimism is horrider. Christians have no business to be pessimists. Don't we believe in the living God? Faith and pessimism are incompatible with one another. To be sure, we Christians are not starry-eyed idealists. On the contrary, we are down-to-earth realists. In other words: We know perfectly well that sin is ingrained in human nature, and sin is also ingrained in human society. I say again: We are not expecting to build a Utopia on earth. That will not come until the second coming of Jesus. But we also know that the gospel has transforming power. It is the power of God unto salvation to everyone who believes. Further, Christ commissions us to go into the world as salt and light.

Let's give up our little prudential compromises

So let's repent of both compromise and pessimism. And let's offer ourselves as agents of change to our Lord Jesus Christ, as salt to hinder social decay and light to shine into the darkness and dispel it. Let's not excuse ourselves by developing a minority complex. Even two per cent can make the difference we long to see. I finish with some simple words from Edward Everett Hale, a nineteenth century American pastor in Boston, Massachusetts:

I am only one. But I am one.
I can't do everything. But I can do something.
What I can do, I ought to do.
And what I ought to do, by the grace of God, I will do.

Endnotes

1 In 1999 John Stott chose to launch his book *Evangelical Truth* (IVP) at the IFES World Assembly, which met that year in Korea. By now aged 78, and occasionally losing his place when he spoke publicly, he said he wondered if it may be his final book. It was a call for a principled evangelical unity, which he wanted to be heard. There is a sense in which it and this book belong together, entrusted to IFES students and graduates as to many Timothys.

2 John Stott expanded as follows: These two texts are regularly misapplied in the church, as if they were written to us. Almost everybody, except evangelical and reformed people, misapplies this text. The Pope applies it to himself and to the Catholic bishops. Liberals apply it to themselves in saying: The revelation of God didn't finish with the Bible, there is more to come, and he is revealing it to us. And Pentecostals also claim that it is applied to them.

These are promises that God made to the apostles. We see this as we look carefully at the text. It is not possible to change the identity of the 'you' in the middle of the sentence. 'All this', Jesus says, 'I have spoken to you while I was still with you. But when the Holy Spirit comes, he will remind you of everything that I have said to you. I have much more to say to you, but you cannot bear it now. But when he comes, he will lead you into all the truth...' Seven or eight times the pronoun 'you' is repeated, and it clearly refers to the apostles on each occasion.

3 2 Thessalonians 3:6,14.

4 Galatians 4:13-14.

5 Bishop Ignatius of Syria, the third Bishop of Antioch, died as a martyr in Rome in 108 AD.

6 An early Christian centre in Anatolia.

7 The 16th century reformers understood this very well. Let me quote from Luther: 'Thus, in his teaching, Jesus

subjects the whole world to the apostles through whom alone it should and must be enlightened. All the people of the world – kings, princes, lords, married men, wise men, holy men – have to sit down while the apostles stand up and teach them.'

8 Linden Kent Memorial Professor of English. At a critical period in literary theory, he drew a clear distinction between 'meaning' (the author's intention) and 'significance' (the reader's judgment). He argued that objective knowledge is not absent in the humanities. This bears on how scripture is viewed by the rising generations of graduates.

9 Rudolf Karl Bultmann (1884-1976), a German Lutheran theologian.

10 There are several biographies of Charles Simeon. John Stott took as the inscription for his own memorial stone the words on Simeon's memorial plaque, in the chancel of Holy Trinity Church, namely words from 1 Corinthians 2:2. A grasp of the influence of Simeon is key to understanding evangelical Anglicanism. Simeon's portrait hangs in Blue Boar House, the offices of IFES and UCCF in Oxford, UK.

11 Charles Simeon's principles of interpretation, which formed John Stott's own, are helpfully summarised by John Benton in *Silhouettes and Skeletons* (Didasko Publishing, 2013). This also includes a brief piece by Oliver Barclay (UCCF General Secretary 1964-1980) on Simeon's forming influence on what is now UCCF.

12 See Deuteronomy 6:4,5; Matthew 22:37; Mark 12:30; Luke 10:27.

13 Ephesians 4:5,6.

14 Revd Prof A M Hunter held the Chair of New Testament and served as Master of Christ's College, University of Aberdeen, until his retirement in 1971.

15 See Luther's 1522 *Preface to the New Testament.* In subsequent editions, this comment was removed (by Luther himself), along with other value judgments on books.

16 Francis Bacon (1561-1626) 1st Viscount of St Alban, Attorney General and Lord Chancellor of England. Despite an aborted political career, his writing remained influential as an advocate and practitioner of the scientific method.

17 Johann or Johannes Kepler (1571-1630), a German mathematician and astronomer, is known as the Father of Physical Astronomy. He described himself as a man of science and a man of God.

18 Psalm 9:10.

19 Harry Blamires (b1916), an Anglican theologian and literary critic, studied under C S Lewis. He was Head of the English Department at King Alfred's College, Winchester, UK, now part of Winchester University. His book *The Christian Mind* gained a wide readership globally and is still in print.

20 This is not to suggest that there is no goodness in unbelievers. We all know 'good' people who are not Christians. Their goodness is as a result of what the Reformers called 'common grace'. That is, God gives good gifts to human beings despite their lack of belief. In this way, the rain falls and the sun shines on the just and the unjust; and unregenerate minds can teach us much, but they cannot teach us deep truths of God's revelation for they do not understand them.

21 Roszak (1933-2011), a graduate of UCLA and Princeton, taught history at Stanford, and the universities of British Columbia and California State.

22 Prof John Seldon Whale (1896-1997), a Congregational minister and academic, taught in Cambridge University and lectured widely in North America.

23 Karl Paul Reinhold Niebuhr (1892-1971), theologian and public intellectual who taught at Union Theological Seminary.

24 Charles Haddon Spurgeon (1834-1892) was here referring to John Bunyan, author of the classic epic *Pilgrim's Progress*. Spurgeon, a fine preacher, a writer, and a man of remarkable wit, served as pastor of London Metropolitan Tabernacle for 38 years, and in his lifetime is reputed to have preached to ten million people.

25 John Stott and a few friends founded the London Institute for Contemporary Christianity (licc.org.uk) in 1982 and he served as a founding director.

26 Robert Neelly Bellah (1927-2013) who coined the term 'civil religion', was of Communist persuasion while an undergraduate at Harvard where he then taught, before moving to the University of California, Berkeley, where he was Elliott Professor of Sociology, Emeritus. In 2000 Bellah received the US National Humanities Medal. He saw trends clearly and, as the citation of his medal announced, he 'raised our awareness of the values that are at the core of our democratic institutions and of the dangers of individualism unchecked by social responsibility.'